ELEPHANTS FROM THE SEA: THE NORTHERN ELEPHANT SEAL

Lynn M. Stone

THE ROURKE CORPORATION, INC.

Vero Beach, FL 32964

Photo Credits:

Library of Congress Cataloging in Publication Data

Stone, Lynn M.
    Elephants from the sea: the northern elephant seal / by Lynn M. Stone
        p. cm. – (Animal odysseys)
    Includes index.
    Summary: Describes the physical characteristics, behavior, and unusual life cycle of this large seal, which lives part of its life on land and part far out to sea.
    ISBN 0-86593-106-2
    1. Northern elephant seal – Juvenile literature.
[1. Northern elephant seal. 2. Seals (Animals)]
I. Title. II. Series: Stone, Lynn M. Animal odysseys.
QL737.P64S76 1991
599.74'8–dc20

                                        90-2360
                                          CIP
                                           AC

CONTENTS

1
ELEPHANTS FROM THE SEA

Elephant seals, named for the trunklike noses of the males, were once called sea-elephants. Their overstuffed snouts are fascinating, but it is the elephant seal's life cycle that is truly astonishing. An elephant seal doesn't look like a mermaid, but it has the same rare ability to live part of its life on land and part far out at sea.

Hauled out on shore, elephant seals look comically out of place. The male, or bull, elephant seal is a brownish-gray mountain of fat. Moving along a beach, his body ripples like Jello. When these part-time creatures of the land return to the sea, however, they are masters of their **environment**, exceptionally skilled, swift, and enduring swimmers.

In its ocean **realm** an elephant seal can outmaneuver a great white shark. It can dive repeatedly, hour after hour, day after day, week after week. Its stamina for swimming and diving is extraordinary. Some of its dives reach depths of 3,000 feet and more, over one-half

Above:
Ashore, bull elephant seals are round mountains of blubber.

mile down into the sea. It can stay submerged for more than 30 minutes.

Little is known about the elephant seal's **odyssey** from shore into the sea, but scientists do know that northern elephant seals travel hundreds of miles. Remarkably, each year they find their way back to familiar home beaches in California and Mexico.

Being an elephant seal means being able to adjust from life on land to life in the water. (Frogs and toads, on a much smaller scale, make the same kind of adjustment.) Being an elephant seal also means being fat. But being fat doesn't bother an elephant seal. In fact, it is the

seal's fat, or **blubber** – up to 1,800 pounds of it – that helps keep it fit. The blubber fills out a seal's skeleton and gives it the torpedo shape that makes for wizardry under water. In water, its fat protects the seal from cold temperatures. When the seal is ashore, its fat saves it from starving. A skinny elephant seal would be a sorry beast indeed.

Healthy elephant seals are built like watermelons, not like bananas. They are the largest seals on Earth, and one of the largest animals of any kind. North-

Above:
A northern elephant seal bull may outweigh its mate by four times.

ern elephant seals measure 15 to 18 feet long and weigh 3,600 to 5,400 pounds. Big bulls weigh considerably more than the largest American cars. The southern elephant seal, a close cousin of the northern elephant seal, weighs up to 8,000 pounds!

Northern elephant seal cows are 9 to 12 feet long and weigh 1,200 to 1,800 pounds. Although they aren't exactly lightweights, they are two to four times smaller than the bulls. Probably no other mammal in the world shows such a tremendous difference between the weights of the sexes.

As you might expect, elephant seals have hefty appetites. They must eat often and in large quantities to maintain their blubber, which can account for up to one-third of their total weight. Large bulls carry blubber in deposits up to six inches thick. Even the smallest elephant seal has at least a one-inch cushion of blubber under its skin.

One of the many astonishing things about these huge animals is that they spend up to four months of the year "dieting." They aren't avoiding food to lose weight, as people who diet do. When elephant seals are ashore, however, they do not eat. These periods are called **fasts**, and during a fast the seal lives on fat reserves.

Elephant seals come ashore to mate, have pups, and **molt**. Molting is the process by which a seal's old skin peels away in patches and is replaced by new skin.

But their real home is the sea. Their bodies are much more agile in the water than on the beach, and the ocean is home for the fish and other **marine** creatures that elephant seals eat.

Above: *Elephant seals must come ashore to mate, have pups, and molt.*

The bull elephant seal's nose is probably of no particular benefit undersea. On land, however, it is a thing of wonder. By the age of eight years, a bull elephant seal's nose droops over its mouth, just as an elephant's trunk does. When the seal raises its two-foot nose and enlarges it through increased blood flow to the region, the animal looks like it has a boxing glove attached to its snout. The nose serves as an echo chamber and amplifier for the bull's trumpeting calls. It also helps establish that he is, indeed, an adult male. Beyond that, **biologists**, the scientists who study living things, aren't sure that this nose has any additional purpose. Female elephant seals have rather short, traditional seal snouts.

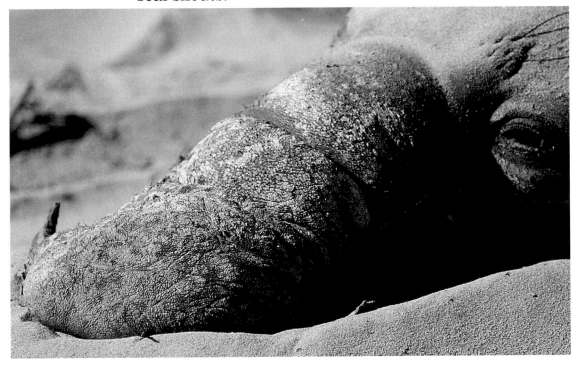

Above:
A bull elephant seal's nose may be two feet long.

Northern elephant seals *(Mirounga angustirostris)* slip ashore to **breed** and molt on several islands off the coasts of Baja California in Mexico and southern and central California in the United States. Their only big mainland **rookery**, a gathering place for breeding, is at

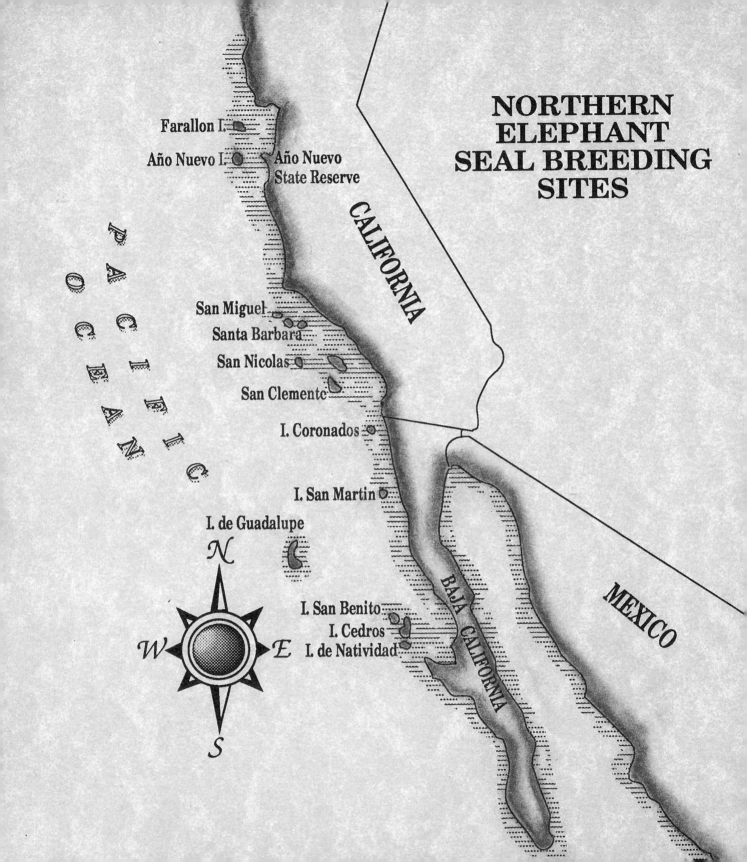

the Año Nuevo State Reserve south of San Francisco. Occasionally a few elephant seals haul out on other mainland beaches.

The range of northern elephant seals at sea is a mystery, because they are rarely seen. They do show up from time to time in the Pacific waters of southeast Alaska and British Columbia.

Far to the south of Mexico and California live the southern elephant seals *(Mirounga leonina)*. They are close cousins of the North American elephant seals. The two types of elephant seals act and look much alike, but the southern elephant seals live in a much colder climate – the icy seas from southern Argentina to Antarctica. Despite their similarities, the northern and southern elephant seals represent two separate **species**, or kinds, of seal.

The northern species has a more elephantlike nose. The southern species is heavier, longer, and capable of more flexibility in twisting its body. There are also minor differences in the skulls and skeletons of the two species.

2
PINNIPEDS

Elephant seals share many characteristics with other seals and walruses. Biologists call seals and walruses **pinnipeds**. This is a particularly special and interesting group of **mammals**. Even though they are air-breathing animals, pinnipeds spend much of their lives in the water, usually an ocean environment. There they are **predators**, hunters of marine animals.

Left:
The elephant seal's ancestors were probably similar in many ways to this sea otter.

Living in the sea has required pinnipeds to develop certain **adaptations**, features that allow them to function in their environment. Millions of years ago, seals were probably land animals, like the great majority of furry, four-legged, milk-producing animals known as mammals. Biologists suspect that the elephant seal's distant ancestors were otterlike animals that lived by the sea. As environmental conditions changed over the years, the seals' ancestors changed too. By developing such adaptations as smooth, torpedo-shaped bodies and

Below:
The West Indian manatee belongs to the sirens, another group of aquatic mammals.

flippers, they were able to spend increasingly more time in the sea, where food was more plentiful. Today pinnipeds generally live along the coasts of cool and cold oceans throughout much of the world. Thirteen species of pinnipeds live in North American waters.

Pinnipeds have kept some of their ties to the land. They are not as completely **aquatic** as two other groups of mammals, the **cetaceans** and **sirens**, which never go ashore. Cetaceans are porpoises, whales, and dolphins. Sirens include sea cows, the dugong, and the manatee, which lives along the Florida coasts. Although they, too, are air-breathing mammals, these animals have no means of locomotion on land. In cetaceans and sirens, the hind legs or flippers found on most mammals have been replaced by broad, flat tails.

The world "pinniped" means "fin-footed," which is a fair description of a flipper. Flippers are the most distinctive **external**, or outer, feature of pinnipeds. Flippers are flattened and webbed hands and feet. In effect, flippers have made pinnipeds swimmers instead of joggers.

One group of pinnipeds, made up of fur seals and sea lions, can rotate its rear flippers forward. Once ashore, sea lions walk on all four flippers. The so-called true seals, including the elephant seal, cannot maneuver their hind flippers forward. They move on land by dragging themselves with their front flippers.

Above:

California sea lions, unlike elephant seals and other "earless" seals, have tiny ear flaps.

Pinnipeds typically have long, round bodies with blunt, whiskered faces. In keeping with the smooth, streamlined look, seals either have no external ears or very small ears. The elephant seal is among the earless group. The sea lions that share the California coast with northern elephant seals have tiny, curled ear flaps.

Pinnipeds range in size from 75 pounds to the four-ton southern elephant seals. All seals have their pups on land or ice, where they form breeding **colonies** of hundreds, thousands, and even hundreds of thousands.

3 BEACH BRAWLERS

After three months at sea, northern elephant seal bulls begin to haul out onto sandy beaches in late November. The urge to mate has gripped the fat, sleek male seals, and they seek out the same beaches of California and Mexico where they have gathered with female elephant seals before. For several days the bulls have the

Right:
Fights between elephant seal bulls at the rookery can be bloody.

Left:
Bellowing by elephant seal bulls often leads to fighting.

beach to themselves, sharing it only with gulls and dark brant geese. The bulls occupy themselves by dozing and challenging each other with blustery roars. Roaring often leads to fighting.

The outcomes of these battles determine the top-ranked, or **alpha**, bulls. For the next three months the alpha bulls become beachmasters – fearless, belching, bellowing fellows with an eye for lady seals. A newcomer may be challenged by the beach lords before he even has a chance to splash ashore. If he is big enough, the bulls on the beach may give him plenty of space to sprawl. Otherwise, a newcomer may be driven into deeper water by a larger bull or forced into a brawl.

Fights erupt on the beach and in the shallows. Fights are frequent and often bloody. Elephant seal bulls have plenty of stomach for fighting. They have been battle-tested since the age of two months, when they fought their first mock battles. Not all bulls survive eight years to reach full adulthood. For the few that do, fighting is just another day at the beach.

Battles in the water resemble duels between giant, thick-necked sea serpents. The seals' backs and hindquarters are submerged, so only their heads, shoulders, and long necks rise above the surface. Bellowing and splashing, the seals smash into each others' chests in a collision of 5,000-pound bodies. They lunge at each other with open mouths and flashing **canine teeth**. Their

Right:
Northern elephant seal bulls duel in water like giant sea serpents.

necks and chests take abuse well. Those jelly roll noses are something else again. A sharp, slashing bite on an opponent's tender nose often ends the battle quickly.

The brawls can be 10-round affairs, too, lasting for a full 30 minutes. By then, one of the bulls has usually had enough punishment and begins to clumsily back away. Reverse gear does not come easily to a 5,000-pound mound on flippers, and backing off doesn't guarantee a noble retreat. The winner sometimes chases and bites the defeated bull.

Despite the bloodshed, these seals rarely suffer major injuries. Their blubber usually protects them from serious wounds. The great shield of blubber on a bull's chest is a thick-skinned quilt of scars from battles past.

The most likely risks for the bulls are injuries to their eyes and jaws. A blind eye or a broken jawbone can eventually lead to the animal's death, since it will make it hard for him to eat properly.

The rookery beach is no place for the timid, especially after cows begin to arrive in late December. The bulls have sorted out their rankings somewhat, but the presence of cows continues to stir the battle instinct and awaken the bulls' urge to mate. The **dominant** bulls – the most powerful animals – will mate most often with the cows. The desire to be with cows is the driving force

Below:
Rookery beaches are no place for the timid.

20

in an elephant seal bull's life at this time. Sometimes that requires another round of blood-letting with a like-minded rival bull. Battles between bulls are more than spectacles; they insure that only the strongest bulls will father the majority of pups. Such selective breeding helps pass the strength of one generation on to the next.

Females flop ashore in groups. The group affords each cow some protection from aggressive bulls. The females are not ready to mate, but they cannot always discourage a bull, especially if a bull singles out one female. The females are pregnant when they come ashore, and they and their unborn pups can be severely injured or killed by the hulking males.

On the high beach, in the company of a dominant bull, the cows have their pups within three to six days after their arrival. For each group of 40 or 50 cows, there is usually one dominant bull. The cows may not like the bull's attentions, but they know that dealing with one dominant male is easier than dealing with several lesser males. So the cows accept the bull, and whenever a low-ranking bull tries to mate with a cow, the cow's alarm cries bring the herd bull charging to her rescue.

The beachmaster cannot usually guard more than 50 cows. Some of them are always departing or arriving, and he has no influence over their travels. If high waves prompt the cows to shuffle elsewhere, the bull resettles with them. If the herd bull lumbers away to chase a bull unnecessarily, a nearby bull will sneak into the herd. So the alpha bull stations himself generally near the center of "his" cows, or **harem**. Three or four lower ranking bulls lounge on the edges of the harem.

This arrangement suits the alpha bull well. He is near any cow that is ready to mate, and when a rival bull approaches the harem, the bulls on the outskirts rush to chase him away or do battle. The alpha bull is thus saved the trouble and loss of energy that would be required if he had to fight off every intruder himself.

Saving energy is important. During their weeks on the beach, the seals fast. They rarely enter the water, and when they do it is to cool off, not eat. Their only **nutrition**, or nourishment, comes from their own body fat. By fasting, bulls avoid missing an opportunity to mate, and females are always available to nurse their pups.

Cows continue to arrive on the beach well into January. About three weeks after a cow has had her pup, she is ready to mate and conceive the pup she will give birth to the following winter. Normally she mates with the dominant bull. Shortly afterward, she leaves the beach and returns to the ocean. The pup remains on shore without its mother. After just four weeks, the bond between the cow and pup has been broken forever.

Below:
While nursing her hungry pup for a month, a female elephant seal loses several hundred pounds.

The females are badly undernourished when they return to the sea. Their coats, no longer sleek and glove-tight, are loose and wrinkled, a size too big. Such is the consequence of the cows' tremendous weight loss. While nursing her pup for a month, a cow may lose up to 40 percent of her weight.

When a cow is ready to leave the rookery, the alpha bull does not interfere. But when she reaches the sea's edge, the lower-ranked bulls cruising the shoreline

may try to mate with her. A bull's attentions to a departing cow, however, draw the interest of nearby bulls. Often fighting erupts and the prize-to-be swims away while her suitors fight to determine only who shall be the biggest loser.

One by one, the bulls begin to leave the rookery in late February. Most of the cows have gone by then, and the bulls' interest in both fighting and females has slackened. Some bulls linger into March, apparently satisfying their need for rest and relative quiet.

In January and February, the rookeries are anything but restful. Life is loud, crowded, and sometimes brief. The cows don't fight, but they nip and bicker like fishwives. Bodies are crowded together and noise is constant. Elephant seal sounds range from booming, deep-throated bellows to hisses, grunts, gurgles, ahs, belches, and less easily described noises. Shorebirds, ignoring the racket, quick-step along the beach and check the dark ribbons of seaweed for morsels of food. The screams of gulls, drawn to the rookery for daily feasts on birth tissue and dead pups, are nearly swallowed by the chorus of seal talk.

For all of its noise and activity, the elephant seal rookery does not have a carnival atmosphere. The seals face constant stress. This is a critical time of year for northern elephant seals. It is the only time during the entire year when they give birth, mate, and ensure the well-being of their species. Bulls are in a dither over cows or approaching rival bulls. The cows have to feed and protect their pups and avoid rampaging bulls. Meanwhile, the energy reserves of both sexes dwindle daily.

4
BEACH BABIES

After the departure of adult seals, the rookeries include primarily groups, or **pods**, of young seals. They are the lucky ones, the pups that have survived. Many of the pups do not live beyond the first month or six weeks of life. Growing up on a sunny beach in California or Mexico sounds much easier than it really is.

From the moment they are born, baby elephant seals face danger. If they are swept into the sea by storm waves, they will drown. If they are separated from their mothers, they will most likely starve. Many are trampled by bulls. In their rushes to combat rivals, elephant seal bulls often crush pups.

A baby elephant seal weighs 65 to 90 pounds. It doubles its weight in less than two weeks, and by the age of four weeks, it may weigh up to 360 pounds. Nevertheless, these butterball pups are no match for bulls that outweigh them by as much as 80 times. That's like a 100-pound person being run over by two large cars at the same time. In some crowded rookeries, as many as one of every three pups dies.

Some deaths occur when a pup is orphaned by a storm or a commotion in the rookery. If the lonesome pup is not recognized by its mother, it may try to attach itself to another cow. Even though mothers and their pups normally do recognize each other after separation, there are exceptions. An inexperienced cow may let an orphan nurse, and occasionally a cow that has lost her own baby will adopt an orphan pup. Generally, however, orphaned pups are bitten and chased away by nursing cows. The pups eventually starve or die from bite wounds.

Born in a woolly, black coat, baby elephant seals fill out their loose skins quickly. A mother seal's milk is liquid butter! During the final week of its four-week

Below:

Elephant seal pups fatten rapidly on a diet of extremely rich milk.

nursing period, the elephant seal pups drink milk that is more than half fat. By comparison, human milk is just two to four percent fat. Cattle produce milk with four percent fat, and whales and porpoises have milk ranging from 25 to 40 percent fat. By producing such rich milk, elephant seals rapidly transfer their own weight and fat directly to their pups.

Seal pups do not have long to be babies. After nursing, they are abandoned when their mothers return to sea. The milk that has been the pups' lifeline is gone. Overnight the pups are **weaned**, taken off their mother's milk. Some of the seals steal milk from cows that are still in the nursery. Young cows are sometimes careless about whom they let nurse. But for the most part, baby seals, like their mothers before them, now have to live on their own body fat.

Without their mothers for warmth and protection, the pups gather together in groups called weaner pods. At first the weaners sleep often, but eventually they begin to enter shallow water. They soon learn how to swim by themselves. Before long, they can dive and stay underwater for 15 minutes. Once their water skills are perfected, at the age of three or four months, the weaners leave the rookery and swim out to sea.

Northern elephant seals can live at least 15 years, but most of them don't. Nearly half of the female elephant seals and eight or nine of every 10 males die before the age of eight.

Right:
Left by their mothers, weaner pups learn to swim in sheltered tidal pools.

Even short-lived elephant seals contribute to the herd, however. Females are usually three when they have their first pup. Males can father pups at four, but they are eight or nine years old before they are strong enough to compete for harem rights.

Many species of young mammals spend several months, or even years, with their mothers. They learn from their mothers, and sometimes from other adults, how to be elk or orangutans or whatever it is they are to be. But elephant seal pups, left on their own at the age of four weeks, have to develop and learn on their own. More amazingly, they have to learn to be elephant seals in two completely different environments – land and sea. How they learn all that they need to know puzzles biologists. Equally puzzling is how these animals find their way back from the sea to the beaches where their lives began.

5
ELEPHANTS IN THE SEA

Biologists know how elephant seals behave on land. Less is known about their behavior as animals of the sea. Elephant seals in the ocean are difficult to follow and observe. They wander over great distances and vanish in long, deep dives to a dark, hidden world undersea.

Elephant seals are seldom seen in the open sea. No one knows how far elephants seals may travel at sea from their rookery beaches. Elephant seals have been sighted in Alaska and British Columbia waters, a long distance from California and Mexico, but these may not represent the longest distances that northern elephant seals travel. Why elephant seals travel great distances is just one of many elephant seal mysteries.

Biologists do know that northern elephant seals are incredible diving machines. They also know that seals dive non-stop, hour after hour, 24 hours a day. The same animals that lie sluggishly on a California beach become workaholics at sea.

Above:

An elephant seal's travels at sea are not well known.

The ability of an air-breathing animal to dive 2,000 or 3,000 feet into the ocean, as elephant seals do, borders on the fantastic. Although sperm whales can dive to 9,000 feet, most sea mammals dive to shallower depths. Dolphins (porpoises), for instance, fish in the 150-foot range, and sea otters hunt in no more than 120 feet of water. But elephant seals have some unique features that permit them the luxury of reaching exceptionally deep places on the ocean bottom.

Basically, the northern elephant seal can stretch the supply of oxygen in its bloodstream far better than most mammals can. The elephant seal can slow its heartbeat from a normal rate ranging from 55 to 120 beats per minute to a range of just 4 to 15 beats per minute. That saves oxygen. By conserving oxygen in its blood, the seal needs fewer breaths, so it doesn't have to surface for air. On long dives, an adult elephant seal can stay submerged for over 30 minutes without a gulp of fresh air.

The elephant seal has a greater volume of blood per pound of body weight than a human. Blood transports oxygen, and an elephant seal's blood has more oxygen-carrying red blood cells than human blood. Also, an elephant seal's body and bloodstream are specially designed to handle the problems associated with the tremendous water pressure of deep dives.

While swimming and diving, the elephant seal powers itself with rear flippers and flexing movements of its body. Its nostrils and ears close tightly like submarine hatches. The seal can't smell or breathe, but it can still hear well. The elephant seal doesn't need its sense of smell underwater, and it rarely needs a breath. Just how important the elephant seal's hearing is undersea has not been determined. Some marine hunters rely on sound waves to reveal the location of **prey**.

6
PREDATOR AND PREY

An elephant seal will never make an Olympic diving team. The seal doesn't dive for sport or play. The elephant seal dives because it must. Most of its prey, deep-water fish and marine **invertebrates**, live in the ocean depths. Few sea predators dive as deep as elephant seals. Presumably, the seals find plenty of food and little or no competition for it.

The ability to dive deep solves the problem of reaching the ocean bottom. Locating the food in deep ocean water is another problem, however, because the sea depths are as dark as caves. The elephant seal has solved that problem with large eyes that see the faintest sources of light. Sunlight doesn't penetrate into extremely deep water, but many animals that live in this dark world have chemicals in their bodies that send out light. Apparently, the elephant seal can focus on these creatures. The seal probably also uses its long whiskers to help locate prey. The whiskers may be sensitive enough to register the vibrations from the movements of prey.

Elephant seals catch prey in their mouths and swallow it whole. Their teeth leave no room for escape. The fearsome canine teeth of elephant seal bulls are as long as six-and-one-half inches, including the roots. Elephant seal teeth are similar to those of land **carnivores**, such as dogs and cats.

Below:
Sleep may not heal the wound inflicted by a shark on this elephant seal bull, but time will.

The prey that elephant seals eat supplies them with energy and builds up their fat reserve. This fat is the source of nourishment during fasts. It is also the seals' source of water. Sea water is too salty for seals to drink, so they rely on the water that their own fat produces.

Because they have to manufacture their own water, water conservation is important to elephant seals. Their bodies have several special adaptations that help them avoid waste in moisture. They have few sweat glands, for example, and their milk and urine contain only small amounts of water.

At times, the predators become prey. Elephant seals are sometimes eaten by great white sharks and by 25-foot long killer whales (orcas), both of which have mouthfuls of teeth that would frighten a tyrannosaur. Young seals are much more likely to be preyed upon than adults.

A great white shark's attack doesn't necessarily kill an elephant seal. Once an elephant seal is aware of a shark, it can outswim the fish. Unfortunately, the shark may be discovered only after it has slashed a chunk of blubber from the seal. Still, seals often survive these maulings.

7
WEATHER-BEATEN OLD SALTS

At various times after the breeding season concludes, the northern elephant seals return to molt on the rookery beaches. Young seals normally molt in April and May. Adult females haul out in May and June. The bulls go ashore in July and August. These visits to the shore

Left:
Molting elephant seals sprawl on the sand like clusters of huge, peeling sausages.

Above:
Seal skin peels away in tattered patches.

are briefer and less stressful than the winter landings. The molting process takes three to four weeks, and during that time the elephant seals sprawl lazily on the sand like clusters of huge, peeling sausages, often lying as still as beach stones.

If you have ever been sunburned and blistered, you have a fair idea of how an elephant seal molts. A molting seal is simply renewing its outer layer of skin by replacing the old with new. It doesn't shed its entire skin like a body glove; snakes do that. Seal skin peels like your sunburn, in dry patches. As the old skin sloughs off, the new layer is revealed.

Molting elephant seals probably leave the sea to preserve their body heat. Otherwise, they could molt while at sea. In the cold Pacific Ocean, the flow of blood to the elephant seal's skin is reduced so that heat can be directed to the seal's insides. When the seal's new skin and hair develop, they require additional blood flow. That means less blood – and heat – is circulated to the seal's internal organs. By hauling onto the beaches, an elephant seal can stay warm internally and provide increased blood to its skin. The air temperature of the

Below:
Molting northern elephant seal bulls on the beach lounge together for warmth, but bulls in the shallow water brawl half-heartedly.

Above:
*Elephant seal
tears bathe
and protect
their eyes.*

beaches is normally warmer than the water, and heat loss is not nearly as great as it would be in the ocean. Furthermore, seals ashore lie against one another for warmth.

During the molt, the same bull elephant seals that were bitter rivals four months earlier lounge together like old seamates. Here and there one seal uses a neighbor's back for a headrest. In typical elephant seal

39

fashion, however, these peaceful moments of slumber and sharing are not without occasional bullying and throaty quarrels. Sometimes the bulls even fight, though half-heartedly, in the shallow water at the shore's edge.

Molting elephant seals look like weather-beaten old **salts**, true sons and daughters of the sea. The patch-work of old skin and new gives the seals a ragged, forlorn appearance. The down-and-out look is heightened by the tears that ooze from the seals' eyes. But the seals aren't crying or looking for sympathy. Their tears are a fluid that bathes and protects their eyes from salt and sand.

Molting seals have an abundance of sand at their flipper tips. Some of the sand reaches their eyes because seals are fond of flipping great clouds of it onto their bodies. The sand showers help shield their backs from the sun. By avoiding some of the sun's direct heat, the seals are able to keep themselves more comfortable on warm days.

After it finishes the molt, an elephant seal looks rather elegant as it slips beneath the waves to begin another ocean odyssey. For the next few months, until late autumn, the elephant seal will presumably live by itself, once again a sleek ocean predator.

Left:
Showers of sand help cool molting elephant seals.

8
SAVING THE NORTHERN ELEPHANT SEAL

Looking at the thriving rookery of northern elephant seals at Año Nuevo State Reserve in California today, you would never guess how close to **extinction** these animals once were. Perhaps the only clue of that is found in the seals' behavior: They are fearless of human observers. In another time, before many laws had been enacted to protect wild animals, the elephant seals' fearlessness made them easy prey for "sealers," as seal hunters were called. The northern elephant seals were nearly slaughtered out of existence. In fact, their total population may have been less than 100 at the turn of the century.

Unlike many of their relatives, elephant seals don't have much hair. Their coats were worthless to seal hunters, but their blubber was valuable. When blubber is boiled, it yields natural oil. Sealers found that a big northern elephant seal bull could be boiled down to more than 200 gallons of oil.

In the 1800s, animal oil had several uses, and elephant seals produced a fine, high-quality grade. Only sperm whales were more highly regarded as a source of oil. Elephant seal oil was used for waterproofing clothes and in the manufacture of soap and paint. It fueled indoor and outdoor lights and also greased machinery.

Until about 1818, elephant seals were overlooked. Ship captains were more interested in whales than seals. As the number of whales decreased, however, many whalers took up seal hunting. The northern elephant seal population tumbled. Thousands upon thousands of elephant seals and other species were killed. By 1870, northern elephant seals had become so rare that there was no profit in hunting them. The few survivors were ignored.

No laws, either in Mexico or the United States, protected the seals. Like the buffalo in the West, seals could be freely pursued and killed. Instead of trying to save the few remaining northern elephant seals, governments forgot about them. Between 1880 and 1884, sealers slaughtered another 419 at San Cristobal Bay and Guadalupe Island, Mexico.

Perhaps most telling about the horrible state of conservation in the 1800s was the Townsend expedition of 1892. Sponsored by the U.S. Department of State, the group was primarily looking for fur seals. During the search, C. H. Townsend was delighted to find eight northern elephant seals at Guadalupe Island, 150 miles at sea. The fact that Guadalupe was Mexican territory did not stand in Townsend's way. He had seven of the seals butchered. The species was doomed, he reasoned, so these animals might as well be "saved" for U.S. museums.

When Townsend returned to Guadalupe Island in March, 1911, he found 125 northern elephant seals, no thanks to his earlier visit. But discovery of the seals meant that the species still had a chance. Mexico acted to give the seals partial protection in 1911 and total protection in 1922. By then, of course, seal oil was no longer in demand. Oil from underground wells had taken its place.

Saved by the changing times, the northern elephant seal populations on remote islands began to increase. By the 1920s, elephant seals once again began appearing off California. The U.S. government soon protected its revitalized elephant seal population. In the winter of 1960-61 the first pups were born at the Año Nuevo Reserve.

Año Nuevo Reserve, which consists of eight-acre Año Nuevo Island and 1,000 acres of windblown shore on the mainland, is certainly the easiest place to see northern elephant seals. The state of California manages the reserve, and thousands of visitors come each year to glimpse the huge elephants from the sea.

Right:

One of the most unusual animal reserves in North America, California's Año Nuevo includes Año Nuevo Island – in the distance – and 1,000 acres of mainland shore.

Northern elephant seals numbered about 10,000 in 1960. Today there are about 100,000, and they have returned to their former haunts from the Farallon Islands south to Island de Natividad off Baja California. Now their greatest threat is the possibility of oil spills, which could destroy them and their marine food supply.

In 1916, biologist Edward Nelson wrote in *National Geographic* that "there is a serious possibility that these strange and interesting habitants of the sea will soon disappear forever." Considering Nelson's gloomy prediction, the return of the elephant seal has been remarkable. But then, the northern elephant seal is a remarkable animal.

adaptation – a characteristic of function, form, or behavior that improves a living thing's chances of survival in its home

alpha – the dominant animal

aquatic – growing or living in water

biologist – a person trained to study plants and animals

blubber – fat, especially in marine mammals

breed – to mate and reproduce

canine teeth – a particular set of sharp teeth

carnivore – a meat eater

cetacean – a group of primarily marine mammals including porpoises, whales, and dolphins

colony – a group of breeding animals of the same kind

dominant – most powerful

environment – the total surroundings in which a plant or animal lives

external – relating to something outside

extinction – the state of no longer existing

fast – to go without food; the time spent without food

harem – a group of females associated with one male

invertebrate – an animal without a spinal column, such as jellyfish, starfish, crabs, and insects

mammal – a furry or hairy four-legged, warm-blooded animal that bears live young and produces milk for them

marine – of or related to the ocean

molt – the loss of fur or feathers

nutrition – nourishment

odyssey – a long journey

pinniped – a group of marine mammals including seals and walruses

pod – a group of animals, especially marine mammals

predator – an animal that kills and feeds on other animals

prey – an animal hunted for food by another animal

realm – the region in which an animal lives and tends to be dominant, its kingdom

rookery – the place at which large numbers of animals gather to raise young

salt – an old sailor, seafarer

siren – a group of aquatic mammals including the manatee of North America

species – a group of animals or plants whose members reproduce naturally only with other plants or animals of the same group; a particular kind of plant or animal, such as a *northern* elephant seal

wean – to remove a mammal from a steady diet of mother's milk

Numbers in boldface type refer to photo and illustration pages.

Elephant seals live on several islands off the coasts of California and Mexico's Baja California for part of each year. It is during this annual period of mating and raising pups that elephant seals can be seen predictably. During the rest of the year, they escape almost all observation by living in the open sea.

Knowing where elephant seals can be found is a beginning. But reaching them can be a major project. Travel to the offshore islands can be dangerous, expensive, and, in some situations, illegal. By far the most convenient place for a close-up look at wild elephant seals is the Año Nuevo State Reserve, part of the California State Parks system. Año Nuevo is about 45 miles south of San Francisco. Here elephant seals have established a breeding colony on the California mainland. If the species continues to prosper and island colonies become crowded, other mainland colonies may appear in the future. But for now, the Año Nuevo site is a wonderfully unique observation site.

The reserve permits visitors to walk about two miles from a parking lot to a beach where they can observe the seals. Rangers discuss the elephant seal's life history and also keep visitors a respectful distance from the seals. A rope keeps people from invading the colony, but the seals sometimes ignore the rope and stretch out on the path.

During the winter breeding season, when the seals are at their boisterous best, visitors show up in such large numbers that observation times are limited to a few minutes. Quotas are in force during the winter, and latecomers may be turned away.

Northern Elephant Seal Site

Año Nuevo State Reserve, CA

Ed. Note: The site listed here does not represent the only place where northern elephant seals may be observed. It is a site that is reliable and has relatively easy access.